The Meaning of Feathers

written by Nicole Suzanne Brown

First Edition 2014

Published in Australia by Spiritual Wisdom Publishing
ISBN 978-0-9922735-1-4
Book design by Spiritual Wisdom Publishing
© 2014 Nicole Suzanne Brown
National Library of Australia
Stay awesome ;)

Other works by Nicole Suzanne Brown

non- fiction -

<u>Passing through Time - Conversations with the Other Side</u>

<u>The Creativity Workbook</u>

<u>The Wee Little Book of The Awesome</u>

The Meaning of Feathers

Give to Get - How to let go to receive all that you need

Fiction -
<u>Pride</u>
Outback Mistress
Phoenix
Home Grown
On the Job

For further information, updates, pre-ordering &
awesomeness visit Nicole at
<u>http://spiritualwisdommagazine.com</u>

ACKNOWLEDGMENTS

Firstly, to my Mum and Dad, you always lift me up, allow me to soar, support, and nurture, and are my shoulders to lean on when life seems unfair. You are the best parents a spiritual girl like me could have. You kick my butt when it needs kicking and kiss my cheek when I'm feeling vulnerable. I love you both so much.

To my beautiful friend Jean. We've been there for each other for twenty-three years and I can't wait to see what we get up to for the next twenty-three. I love you chicky. Hugs to T&T!

To my fellow squishies at Spiritual Wisdom Magazine & Facebook Page.

A HUGE thank you to each and every one of Nicole's ARC Angels! Thank you for being awesome, and for coming along with me on my journey. I couldn't ask for better fans! ! *GROUP SQUISHY HUGS*

And of course thank you to the Universe, God, Spirit, who creates such magnificent miracles every day, so that we can always remember ALL IS ONE, IS ONE.

DEDICATION

To Richard,

For being my muse throughout the writing of this book.
And for reminding me constantly that life is way too short
to be stressing about the small stuff,
and that miracles occur with every breath we take.

Contents

Chapter 1. How to use this book:

The information in these pages is for you to learn, grow, express and create your own pathway to your own spirituality.

Whether you have been walking on your spiritual path for eons of time or just stepped forward, the information received was out of a need, and urge from the readers of Spiritual Wisdom Magazine to learn more about what feathers mean, and why they sometimes magically appear.

Are they here to teach us something about ourselves?

Can feathers hold messages for us, that can unlock healing and change?

Can they help with creativity and bring messages from beyond time and space?

I believe they can.

I believe they do.

And by the end of this book, you will too.

Nicole Suzanne Brown

July, 2014

Chapter 2. **Feathers and Flight - What it all means.**

I have always searched for the meaning of life. My earliest memory is that of a little curly blonde haired girl asking the tough questions, that curly blonde haired girls really shouldn't be asking. When all my friends where off with their barbie dolls or drooling over boys, there I was nestled among the adults listening to their stories, sharing my own and asking why they felt the way they did, and why do things happen to some people and not others?

It is why at the age of twenty-one I quit my job, leaving just enough money to buy a plane ticket, and be living in an Indian Ashram for three weeks among others twice my age, but no less inquisitive.

Little did I know that in my late twenties I would be living and breathing those same questions with the <u>sudden death of my brother Jason</u>.

Jay's death took me further inward on my spiritual pathway where visions of molecular energy would play in my mind, dancing and swirling to the emotions of the people near me. It was a lonely path and even tho' I sought out comfort from those who never had my best interest at heart, I always came back to the source, to knowledge, to creativity and writing, expression and mystery.

I believe that we are each given a gift to share with the world. Be that a listening ear or a brilliant singing voice, the gift of writing or the muse of a writer, we all have the unique ability to inspire and be inspired by.

I also believe that we are given the answers to every question we ever posed or dared mutter out loud. These answers may come in the form of words or writing, songs or scriptures. They may also come from our natural world in the form of fauna and flora. The Animal Kingdom in all its glory has its own spiritual connection to the Earth and her surroundings. Are we so blind in our search that we do not look towards nature for the answer?

If only we trusted our own instincts, our inner voice, our soul, closed our eyes and truly believed we are receiving an answer.

We could stop searching, for there lying at our feet nestled in a pile of rocks, perched against a broken stair, the Universe is talking to us, guiding us, asking us to trust, to open up to the possibility of Universal guidance.

Do you dare believe you are being guided?

Do you trust your instincts enough to allow the answers to what you are looking for, asking about, to be answered in the form of an energy so insignificant as a feather?

For eon's Native people, those connected to Mother Earth, have believed in the power of flight and the power of feathers. Many people have dreamt of flying and this signifies a freedom in an area of their life that they want to bring to another's life. It also is significant in those who are going through a spiritual growth and letting go of old ways, embracing the new energy of lightness and positivity.

Dreaming of a feather symbolises a renewal in Universal trust, instinctual energy beginning to stir and (depending on the colour), a healing on a physical/spiritual side taking place.

That you were in the right place at the right time for a feather to appear in your life shows that you are ready, and able, to take control of your life, choose differently, expand your horizon and, more importantly, allow yourself to truly be swept up in the magic of the Universe that is energy. All powerful. All knowing. All loving energy.

I believe, first and foremost, that when a feather appears, whether it be lying at your feet or gifted from the heavens, you are being reminded in a very unique way that you are loved, that you are guided.

You are here for a purpose. You know this. Otherwise you wouldn't acknowledge a feather if it appeared to you. And I will go even further and say, you will not even be in the energy of receiving one in the first place.

This is not to say that because you haven't received one before, you were on the wrong path, a bad person, but more importantly, that you were doing the best you can with the best you had at the time. Now, the Universe is showing up for you, giving you signposts, gifting you Universal messages that are unique for you, and you alone.

We, each and every one of us, has a need to be comforted, to be acknowledged. To know deep within us that our prayers are not only being heard, but answered. That, I believe, is the beautiful gift that a feather represents.

From an animal that can touch the Earth and the Sky, feathers represent freedom, expression, spirituality, higher consciousness, higher learning, Universal love, guidance and teachings.

You are on the right path. Allow the Universe to guide your way.

Chapter 3. The Spiritual and Physical Meaning of Feathers:

So is there a spiritual and physical meaning to finding a Feather? I believe there is. There are so many messages involved when a Feather is gifted to you, and one of the most important is acknowledging if the message is a Spiritual meaning or a Physical meaning.

In other words, when you found the Feather, did you find it on the left hand side of your body or the right hand side of your body?

If the feather appeared on your LEFT:

This indicates a very strong SPIRITUAL message for you. Your higher self has brought you to this very moment to receive the message you are about to receive. Understand that this message is for your SOUL, your spiritual self, the shadow side of your nature, the dreamer and the lover within you.

The message is being sent to you FROM YOUR soul TO YOUR soul. You planned this moment in life. You planned to receive this sign, this message right now at this moment to move you into the best place your life could be. Acknowledge the message with pure unconditional love. Read the Spiritual Meaning and Affirmation section.

If the feather appeared on your RIGHT:

This indicates a very strong PHYSICAL message for you. The Universe, God, Spiritual Guides or those of our loved ones that have passed before us, are gifting you a message so that your physical side, your body, mind and emotional side can heal, move on from the past and step forward to a brighter, healthier, happier and joy-filled future. Read the Physical Meaning and Affirmation section

Chapter 4. Feathers and The Body - How they affect your physical and spiritual bodies:

In my first book <u>Passing Through Time - Conversations with the Other Side</u>, I spoke with my brother Jay extensively on how we here on Earth can heal the human body. He spoke of 'The GOD-Seed", that energy we call Soul, Spirit, Existence or just plain ol' Me, Myself and I.

So how can we heal our physical body by using feather energy? First, here is Jay explaining The GOD-Seed to me in <u>Passing Through Time - Conversations with the Other Side</u>:

The GOD-Seed

Jay, you speak about the GOD-Seed. What exactly is that?

It is what drives us as individuals to search for and be the best soul we can ever be. We are all part of GOD, the ultimate intellect with energy that lives within everything - every single molecule, cell and life everywhere. Nothing at all is separate from this immensely loving energy.

The GOD-Seed is such an integral part of every being. In human beings it is the energy that is located exactly on your navel, (not to be confused with your solar plexus).

It is actually embedded inside the solar plexus region. The GOD-Seed is similar to a ball of energy, always oscillating, neither right nor left, up nor down.

Once you accept who you are and begin to search for why you are, this energy then begins to activate and evolve into the time continuum symbol of eternity.

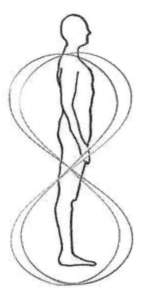

The energy evolves or moves through the root chakra, towards the back and then up to the base of the neck, down through the throat, thymus and solar plexus, then back into the root chakra in a continuing cycle.

Once the body becomes accustomed to the energy that is oscillating through, within and around it, the energy then begins to vibrate at a more rapid molecular structure. This movement initiates the start of your spiritual search (or 'quest' as we call it here where I am).

Because the body is vibrating at a more rapid, 'clearer' energy, more energy is then able to move towards, through and around it. This in turn oscillates and generates more and more divine visions, gifts and learning. Once the being is accustomed to that energy and begins to look within more closely, the energy again surges, oscillating in rapid succession.

The GOD-Seed begins to evolve and move in greater and greater oscillations, encompassing the whole of the human body -

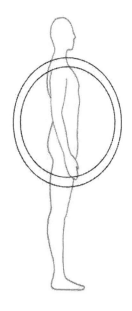

Divine search of self begins. This affects root chakra, grief point (small of back), energy of self-worth and purpose (between the shoulder blades), throat chakra, thymus, sternum and solar plexus.

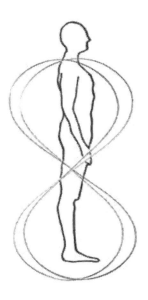

Divine search begins to encompass all life's lessons and manifestations of thought. All of the body's central energy points oscillate at a divine vibrational molecular structure.

Now to begin to evolve to and move into an awareness of your GOD-Seed intellect, you need to first acknowledge the divine within your 'self'.

Practices of conscious breathing and movement enable you to recognize the body's energy and the majestic way it lives, breathes and grows. This is achieved through learning of the most integral and intricate part of energy of self.

Music plays an intricate part in reconnecting you to your GOD-Seed soul. Tribal and primitive music (e.g. African, Negro, Aboriginal, Maori), enables you to concentrate on the first stage or structure of the GOD-Seed.

The drums of the music allow you to locate the primitive energy of the GOD-Seed. Re-connection with the Earth from where you are born is the first structure of the GOD-Seed.

I am playing the soundtrack to the movie "Power of One". Rain has just begun to pour outside and the trees are moving with the strong wind.

Yes, connection with the Earth is important. You are born upon the Earth, but your connection with the Earth is so important.

Connection to the Earth enables the remembrance of gentle strength, letting you realize that the divine plan of ALL IS AS IT SHOULD BE (that is, in constant movement).

Through constant movement comes constant learnings and teachings. Once you re-establish your connection with the Earth, find the awe and majestic beauty that surrounds you and recognize that it also lives and breathes inside of you.

The constant drum beating and Earth chanting awakens the GOD-Seed to evolvement. Therefore, become like a child who dances in the rain. Reconnect yourself to everything, cleansing and celebrating, moving and oscillating with the energy around you. Allow the energy to move through and around your body, recognizing and being in awe of the majestic energy of freedom which fills your very being.

Once through discipline and practice you have begun to establish the re-connection of remembrance within yourself, you will then evolve (and move) into a newer, cleaner energy. During the practice of conscious breathing and movement (achieved through Tai Chi, Chi Gung and other similar arts), you will feel a shift begin. Old thoughts and feelings will resurface which have lain dormant in your solar plexus.

The energy you are now working with (and not against, as you may have been), searches for energy vibrations like itself. As this energy revitalizes the root chakra and the grief point, you will find 'movement' occurring in various issues in your life. This could be to do with sexual issues and memories moving through to grief issues, the energy begins to oscillate through the small of your back, resurfacing remembrance that you are indeed not alone and letting go of old ideas of who you are and what the world is.

The energy then evolves to the area between your shoulder blades. Feelings and thoughts of your self-worth and purpose in your own life and others will surface. Allow all feelings to come. Remember no feelings are good or bad - only feelings.

Once the energy is cleaner and clearer, the GOD-Seed then moves through to the base of your neck. Feelings and thoughts about your connection with yourself and family comes into progress of a spiritual nature. An acknowledgment of the learning and teachings of all paths, with no-judgment and no-expectations, begins to move through your entire soul.

As the energy once again becomes cleaner and clearer, it then evolves to the throat area. Feelings of stifled conformity surface and the energy begins to vibrate at a different molecular structure.
Your voice may become softer, yet stronger due to the energy. Allowing yourself to speak about your experiences, feelings, movements, and thoughts will then enable a 'cleaner' energy to resonate within yourself.

Energy then moves to the sternum at the front of your body. Feelings of guilt re-surface as well as self-consciousness and stress. Allow these feelings and thoughts, which are congested in this area, to re-surface. This will bring on the energy of release and uninhibited awe.

The energy then moves through to the solar plexus.

Feelings and thoughts about lost opportunities and misjudged experiences surface. Allowing the energy of these issues to re-surface enables you to clear and become confident again of your body's natural ability to sense or predict experiences that will ensure growth of your individual intellect.

As the GOD-Seed evolves through the body, allow all feelings and thoughts to come to the surface. This will ensure that you are resonating with the energy of the GOD-Seed.

The GOD-Seed, if you have a need to visualize, is seen as a golden orb, brilliant in light and oscillating at an infinite vibrational structure - It never diminishes. One area of the body is not brighter than the other. The color does not change - for it is all colors and none.

However, if you do visualize a color, take notice of the color and feel how the color resonates with you.

Remember - darker colors are not negative, nor are bright, positive. All is One, is One.

Now once the GOD-Seed has oscillated through these particular energy structures within the body and the energy has become cleaner and clearer, the energy then begins its rapid formation of growth.

The GOD-Seed begins to expand, allowing new experiences to become drawn to this particular energy field. In this expansion comes great movement and within this movement, comes greater awareness of the body's Soul purpose or desire of intellect -

First stage of GOD-Seed oscillation Structure.

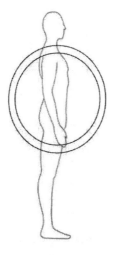

Second stage of GOD-Seed oscillation structure.

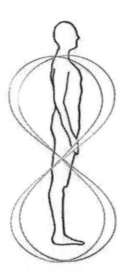

The second stage of the GOD-Seed oscillation structure moves, (or moves into), the energy points of the body's vibrational structure.

Still evolving through the sacral, lower back, shoulder blades, throat, sternum and solar plexus areas, the GOD-Seed stretches or evolves into a larger area, always obtaining new energy and experiences.

These new areas include the thighs, knees, ankles and feet of the human body.

Notice that these physical structures are what allows you to move forward, backward and sideways. They are also your body's way of showing you the primal need of balance within and around your life.

Once the GOD-Seed becomes one again with its natural self, (the GOD-Seed placement centre in the solar plexus region), the energy (intellect), then evolves through the thigh area of the body.

Feelings of strength and individualization will come to the surface. A large portion of self-worth issues are held in your knee and ankle area.

Your thighs represent the feelings of self-empowerment and self-control. Overall balance is maintained by the GOD-Seed evolving through, within and around your thigh area. The overall balance pertains to your life and how you judge it.

You may feel cramps in your thighs and your sciatic nerve (an unconscious control point of movement), will become activated and, in most cases, agitated. Allow the feelings of free movement to sweep through your thighs as you gather strength through knowledge and self-worth.

Now, the GOD-Seed evolves through, within and around the knee area. Feelings of restricted direction (in emotions and the living of our lives), are stored. The feelings of 'not aspiring to the best of your ability' bring through the energy of conformity, stagnation and procrastination.

Allow all feelings, memories and emotions to come to the surface. Remember no feelings are good or bad - just feelings.

The GOD-Seed then evolves through, within and around the shins and ankles. Again we store emotional issues of conforming to others' opinions of our life in this area.

Your ankles hold this key of flexibility and learning through directional balance and movement. Allow the pure energy of self-expression through 'taking charge' of responsibility of your life's direction.

Next, the GOD-Seed moves to your feet. Here it circles and embraces itself through the knowledge of self-power and realistic memories and dreams of your own life. Your feet are your grounding energy. They are what connects you to the realization of who you are and what you are becoming.

The feet store memories of intellect bias, through conformity and lack of good judgment. The energy of having lived your life as you see fit.

When the GOD-Seed evolves/moves through the feet, it reawakens the primal need for connection and stability in your life. Once feelings of such emotions have been cleaned and cleared, the GOD-Seed moves through, within and around the back of the leg, encompassing the calf muscles, the back of the knee joint and the hamstrings.
All of these energy structures in the body are interconnected with issues or feelings of gentle movement. Stiffness is the result of over-compensation and the need to conform to other people's opinions about your life.

By clearing these emotional blockages, you will find a resurgence of gratitude for other people's actions and will re-establish empowerment of movement in your own life and lifestyle.

The GOD-Seed then evolves through, within and around the buttocks. Here, stifled emotions are stored in relation to severe loss of self-worth. This area also registers issues which relate to holding onto instead of moving through, with the creativity and the character of the embodied soul (your personality). The buttocks are close to the grief spot and enable you, through creative practices, to move into the feelings, thoughts and emotions of strength, balance and self-acknowledgement.
Once the GOD-Seed intellect has become one with its natural self, the GOD-Seed begins to oscillate at a more rapid vibrational structure. Similar to the first and second stage of remembering and clearing the emotions, thoughts and feelings of self-esteem, balance and movement (directional and emotional) will re-surface.

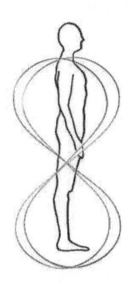

The third stage begins to envelop the intellectual molecular structure of the soul-body. This stage envelops or evolves to and into, the molecular structure of the breath channel (the third eye, crown and over-soul portion of the human body).

With the GOD-Seed expanding its energy (intellect) through the body's central nervous system and the energy centers within and around the body, the THIRD stage (or structure) evolves, through, in and around the breath channel.

This breath channel is located above the throat energy centre (or chakra as it is widely known), encompassing the jawbone, mouth, nose and sinus area of the body.

Feelings of restricted emotions or self-confronting emotions are primarily held in these energy centers of the human body. The sinus area is a centre which enables the free-flowing of emotions, allowing the body to eliminate mucous (or congested emotions). Blocked sinuses symbolize unshed tears.

The GOD-Seed evolves through all the energy centers of the breath channel simultaneously. When the energy of the breath channel is cleared and cleaned, the GOD-Seed then evolves through, into and around the third eye centre.

This centre establishes the soul's desire for inward expression of the outward life being lived, i.e., visions of a celestial and/or intellectual structure occur.

The third eye is the remembrance energy structure of the human body. The link between the GOD-Seed primal centre and the third eye structure of the human body, when established, is an integral symbol of the human connection to the GOD-Within and the GOD-Without (the GOD outside of self).

Feelings of nausea and tension headaches or migraines are an established physical link with the GOD-Seed reconnection with the third-eye. Feelings of how 'small' you are, compared to the outside world, will resurface.

The divine plan of reconnection with all things great and small has an important remembrance with the human body's ability to comprehend the intellect in its entirety.

Reconnecting with the feelings and thoughts that 'nothing is impossible' and 'there is more to living than the life I have previously been living', allows the GOD-Seed energy to oscillate at a rapid vibrational molecular structure.

Images of light flashes and colors will become visible around material and physical structures. Once focused upon and learnt, these insights will help with the body's own healing.

Next, the GOD-Seed proceeds to the crown energy structure of the human body. Located in the middle of the skull, this energy's primal structure is for the releasing or elimination of unused energy that the body, soul and GOD-Seed generate.

Cleaning and clearing this energy structure enables the insight of abundant health throughout the body. Feelings and thoughts related to constriction (and the restricted use of the body's energies), will resurface.

Through re-balancing and remembrance of the GOD-Seed and the primordial flow of that energy, these restrictions may be cleaned and cleared. As a result, the life of the individual will be able to vibrate or gravitate to a less dense energy and health will improve (through intellect and remembrance). A pure sense of self and divinity will emerge. Therefore, you can see, that this is the flow or evolvement of the GOD-Seed soul. By remembering always that the soul encompasses the body (the body does not encompass the soul), you will be led to a more direct sense of health, well-being and self-control in your life and your destiny.

Remember also that the GOD-Seed's evolvement is ever-growing and ever-lasting. No soul is without a GOD-Seed, and no soul is purer or cleaner than another. The particular evolvement of your GOD-Seed is as individual as your breath.

Through all of eternity the GOD-Seed is evolving and moving into less and less dense energy, always finding and remembering the divine plan and that of the individual's divine plan.

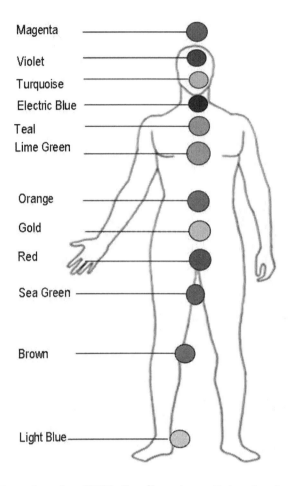

Magenta

Violet

Turquoise

Electric Blue

Teal

Lime Green

Orange

Gold

Red

Sea Green

Brown

Light Blue

Remember also, that the GOD-Seed's primordial color is that of none and all. This is not to be confused with the colors (and vibrational molecular structure) of the energy centers through, within and around the body (the chakras).

These colors or chakras are ever changing and ever oscillating in vibration color wheels. Once you breathe in, the colors become more dense and brighter. Once your breath is released, the colors become less dense and pastel in hue (color).

The wheels (energy centers), oscillate in every direction depending upon the individual and what needs to be learnt in the physical. The wheel may feel or be visualized going clockwise or anti-clockwise. Neither is right or wrong, but indeed perfect for that individual.

Grief Spot situated at small of Back

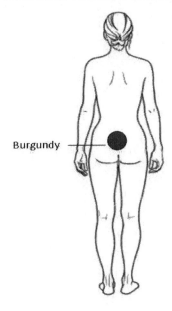

Burgundy

Once the realization of the GOD-Seed is established or remembered, the energy wheel begins to oscillate (move into), the vibration of the GOD-Seed. Again, the direction of movement is not to be judged. Neither left, right, up or down is considered more or less evolving than the other.

Once the GOD-Seed is embedded into the individual growth patterns and the individual Vibrational Molecular Structure is established and oscillating at a rapid vibration, the energy structures (chakras) begin to evolve into the colors of all. All colors oscillate at every energy structure, enabling the energy of intricate colors to weave into the movement of the GOD-Seed.

Again, once this structure of remembrance and reconnection is established, the breath of the body oscillates the colors of energy. Breathing in, the colors become more dense/brighter and by releasing the breath, the colors become less dense/pastel in hue.

We are all immortal. Every living organism on this Earth, indeed included in this Universe, has survived and reached immortality.

Our memory-based intellect has evolved to such an awesome power that lives, locations, rituals, experiences; memories are recorded in everyone's blueprint. If you are affected by anything, you have reached immortality.
You are evolved into it. There has never been a search for immortality, for immortality has never been lost, nor has it ever been something to look up at, but merely was evolved at in a particular time and space.

Everything that is born of energy - whether that is dense, fragmented or pure energy, has evolved into its own immortality. Energy has trace patterns that vibrate at a particular rate, differing from all others. Like human DNA, this energy is unseen by the eye, cannot be touched (therefore cannot be taken), but can be tapped into.

Once focused upon, the energy of anything can be brought forward to a particular time and space, tapped into and harnessed so information and technology will never be lost but grow, as it is continuing to do at such a rapid state in the early 21st Century. Why? Because humans' DNA is changing to a more constant emotional, unified consciousness.

Like atoms in a cell separate, they energize themselves, their surroundings, harness together, vibrating at the same speed, same rate, they now effect and affect everything.
Once only using one third of its own true power, now generating power at a phenomenal rate, affecting itself, stimulating power, growing, vibrating as 'free energy'.

If you are remembered you are Immortal.

Photographs, recorded messages, video, and memories, link immortality to a particular place, to a particular person.
On a more metaphysical level looking beyond material, physical anomalies, fingerprint, aromas, smells, DNA, energy transference patterns, all can be traced, all can be tapped into, to learn from, teach from, a sound base of facts of memories, now your own, stimulating intellect, causing experiences, memories.

Remembered learning's create Immortality. (excerpt Passing through Time).

When a feather appears in your life, there are so many varying degree's of messages that you are receiving. As we discussed before, there is not only the physical and spiritual meanings, but also (and most importantly) what is happening in our emotional body.

Using a Feather in your physical healing can bring a unique vibration into your life. You are YOUR OWN healer. Using the book as a guide, and holding the feather in your hand, notice which colour of the feather corresponds closely with the colour of the Chakra in the illustrations previously shown.

Is this exactly where you have been feeling that a healing needed to take place? Have you had aches and pains in the area of the body that the colour of the feather represents?

Using the GOD Seed technique (moving in a figure 8), bring the feather to the area needing healing and then away from the body.

If your illness/aches and pains are a new ailment, bring the feather towards you and then away from you in a figure 8.

If, however, the aches and pains are an old injury, illness or disease, hold the feather close to your body and then in a figure 8 pattern bring the feather OUT then IN.

The difference in the two techniques? Bringing the feather towards you is bring in new fresh energy from the Universe, God, Spirit.

Bringing the feather from you first, is symbolising the illness/disease leaving your body, giving it back to the Universe, God, Spirit to heal.

Once you do this for 6 days straight, THEN, bring in the feather towards you. Visualise LIME GREEN - the vibrational energy of new life.

Chapter 5. **What does it mean when:**

Many messages in our lives, come to us in the most unexpected ways. And when you think about that, what better way is there than a lovely unexpected message and gifting from above?

So, what is the meaning behind these messages? Is there any significance at all in not only the colouring of the feather but where we find it?

I believe there is. I believe that everything around us is a message from the Universe, God, and Spirit. I believe this is what is meant by 'we are not alone', and 'we are always guiding you'. I believe if we truly looked within, worked out our emotions BEFORE we acted upon them, that we wouldn't need any outside influences to guide us. We after all are ONE with EACH OTHER. ALL IS ONE IS ONE.

But, until that moment that we truly listen to our own inner voice, inner guidance, let's celebrate the fact that we have planned this message, and received it loud and clear.

So, what does it truly mean when:

You see a feather falling from the sky?

You are being asked to stop and take notice of your surroundings and what kind of energy and people you are surrounding yourself with.

Many times in our lives we look towards the heavens to ask for guidance and help and the symbolism of a feather falling towards you is a strong reminder that you have no control over a situation OTHER than being true to yourself and the greater good of all involved.

Are you truly being the best person you can be right now? Is there a situation you are involving yourself in that you have been asking for guidance with?

Go through this guide to find the Colours of Feathers, to find the one that you have noticed.

Then ask yourself these questions:

Am I ready to accept guidance and divine intervention for a question I have wanted answers too?

Am I allowing myself to feel pure love from the Universe that I can then give to myself?

Am I ready to accept healing, guidance and financial abundance from the Universe by truly believing in the sign-posts and messages I am receiving?

Find that a Feather lands on you?

Heaven is literally reaching out and touching you. A guidance and answer to your prayers is happening. A loved one that has passed is right beside you. Close your eyes. Breathe deeply. Allow any feelings and thoughts to come to you right at that moment.

Are you being guided to rest?

Are you being guided to forgive others, as well as to forgive yourself?

Is there a word, phrase, name that continues to be present in your mind?

What colour is the feather? Your loved one is healing you, raising your vibration to one of health, not fear. Raising your energy to one of happiness not loss and loneliness.

Be still and know that you are loved.

Find a Feather in your house?

A spiritual visitation has taken place.

Be aware of the colour of the feather that has presented itself (see Colours of Feathers etc,. for the meaning), and on what side (left, or right) of the room it was found in.

If the feather was:

Just inside the front door: A new cleansing has taken place. Happiness, joy and laughter are surrounding all those that reside in the house. Using a smudge stick/incense of your choice (I prefer Nag Champa) cleanse your front door by using the Tune in and Tune out guide.

In the lounge room: Comfort and peace-filled energy are coming to you. Communication will flow more fluidly, heated arguments will dissipate. A calm, loving space is being created.

In the kitchen: A body detox/cleanse is taking place. Take notice of what you are nurturing and feeding your body. You may go through a healing/health clearing within the next 7 days. Drink warm water with a squeeze of lemon throughout the day to help your body eliminate toxins. A letting go of old, chipped glassware and containers is needed. Clean your kitchen out to clean your body. Archangel Raphael is near.

In the bedroom: Take notice and be aware of your dreams. You are being visited while you sleep, and given the answers to questions you can't bring yourself to speak out loud. Ask for Archangel Michael to cut the ties of insomnia and worry, stress and mistrust. A loved one is visiting. Is there a recent anniversary of someone's passing coming? This visitation is filled with pure love, pure bliss. Know that you are loved. Know that you are guided.

Just outside the back door: A visitation has occurred, a clearing of the past has happened. Have you moved furniture lately? Resolved issues? This visitation symbolises a renewal of healthy, happy energy. A letting go of the past. An old grudge let go of.

Take notice of the colour and become aware of which area of your body and life this is a direct symbol for. Take a broom, and with the energy of the colour and visitation, 'sweep' away any residual energy that may be lurking.

Find a feather on the Car?

Protection. Have you been driven to frustration lately? Driven mad by a situation or a person? You are being guided to take back control of a situation.

On the front of the car:

A keen sense of awareness is needed. Focus. Goal setting and plans being made. Take notice of the little things. Be alert and prepared. You are being guided to give clear signals of what you want and when you want it.

Be precise. Be clear in your mind and clear in your speaking. This is your time now to speak your mind. Do it with love. Be Kind.

On the top of the car:

Higher protection. A loved one that has passed is close by. Have you anxiety over a near miss lately? Ask Archangel Michael to be present when driving, and when all are in your car. You are being guided to have faith that everyone one is looked after, everyone is loved. Pay attention to the songs around you. A message is coming.

On the back of the car:

You are being guided to let go of the past. The past no longer serves you. You are dragging the past behind you, in conversations and in everyday life. Allow the Universe, God, Spirit to clear the stress and anxiety of 'what happened when', away for good. Be aware of the conversations that you have been having with yourself and with others. Clear your feelings, cleanse your thoughts. Let it all go. The future is so much brighter.

On the wheel of the car:

You are being guided to tread carefully with a situation or relationship. Are you being steered in the right direction? Do you feel that you are in control of what is happening or are other peoples energies disrupting your own?

A financial situation needs closer inspection. Be careful that you are not being taken advantage of. A doormat energy could be present. Are you allowing someone to walk all over you.

(Take notice if it is the front or back wheel. Read front of car and back of car after reading).

On the beach?

You are being guided to release something back to the Universe that wasn't yours in the first place. Was there a situation that you took control of that you should have stepped back from? Have you felt that you are no longer needed, so have created a situation where people need your advice, your energy, your finances?

It is time to let go and let God. Allow the Universe to guide you, have faith, trust and patience. You are loved and needed. Allow the Universe to show you the way. Breathe and just let go.

On Water?

You are being guided to express your most vulnerable emotional side. Allowing yourself to feel the emotions as they bubble up, releases the energy that you have been holding onto so long. It is ok to be vulnerable.

You are being guided to acknowledge the strength in tears, the strength in asking for help. There will be times in the next few days, that anger may come. Let it come, for when anger subsides, the tears will flow. This is what is needed now. Emotion and emotional cleansing and clearing.

In a tree?

You are being asked to go 'out on a limb' for a situation to gain fruition. You are being guided to stretch your limits, push yourself higher, think outside the box. Your goals and dreams are within reach. You just need to apply a limit more effort to reach them.

On Stairs?

- walking UP stairs -

You are being guided to look to your future with a positive energy. Your loved ones are stepping on the path with you, moving the obstacles out of the way so that you will achieve all your hopes, dreams and goals.

Shake off the shackles that hold you back, be positive in every area of your life (thought, word and action), and recognise from this day forward that you will BE guided to be in the right place at the right time. You have paid your dues. It is time to celebrate!

- walking DOWN stairs -

You are being asked to slow down and take stock of what you have achieved in your life so far. There is something holding you back, and the loved ones that have passed are asking you to trust them, to give them your burdens, your stress.

Sit with the thoughts that come to you, acknowledge them, love them for what they were, a lesson in life, an experience that allowed you to be in this very moment right now. Then, with the energy of the loved ones that have passed, shake off the energy, lift it up and out of your body (use the healing figure 8 technique), and breathe easy. The hard times are behind you. It is time to step into a new energy of your life.

Chapter 6. Feather colours and their Physical/Spiritual Meanings:

With this chapter, you will find the Colour of the Feather that you have found or been 'gifted', along with the Physical meaning, Spiritual meaning and Affirmations for both.

If you have found a Feather that has more than one colour, read through the meaning of the predominant colour first, then the second and third colours etc,.

For example: If you have been gifted a Black Feather with a Purple tinge or stripe, read through the Black Feather meaning and then the Purple meaning.

You will find that both and/or all these meanings are perfect for the situation that you are in. You have been gifted this particular coloured Feather for a reason. Choose to see each and every message available to you with an open and grateful heart.

If you choose to, you could write down the messages and affirmations and use them from the time of a Full Moon to a New Moon. This energy is a high vibration that enables change, expansion, growth and Universal guidance.

SWAN FEATHER

PHYSICAL MEANING

You are being asked to slow down, that you are protected and very much looked after. You are being guided to acknowledge the peace and beauty within you, that which you share with others in your touch, and the words you choose. You are a healer on an emotional level and your calming presence de-stresses any situation that you are in. Know this. And allow the inner turmoil that you are feeling about someone else's life dissipate. You bring with you the protection they need.

Affirmation: "I am at peace. I am protected on all levels of body, mind and soul. I am peace-filled and loved so much. I love receiving protection and love and in turn give it back to the Universe tenfold".

SPIRITUAL MEANING

You are being lifted and embraced by those who have passed before you. Your physical, emotional and mental bodies are being healed by those who have always guided you in your life. It is time to acknowledge the beauty you bring to the world.

You have worked so hard to get to where you are, relax and be guided. Your life plan is littered with gold and Universal signposts. Be still and know that you are loved.

Affirmation: "I am so grateful for the beauty in my life and the love that constantly surrounds me. I am so blessed that the Universe guides me to where I need to be at exactly the right time for the highest good of all. I love that I am protected fully and express life creatively".

EAGLE FEATHER

PHYSICAL MEANING

You are being asked to step back in a situation and look at it from a distance before making a decision. Find the strength in weighing up your options before you make a firm decision. You are being guided to trust in the Universe, God, Spirit. Have faith that you will not be alone, you will always be protected. Stay still. Breathe. Then make a decision.

Affirmation: "I am so grateful that I have the gift of insight. I am blessed that I allow my soul to guide me, and acknowledge the Great Spirit within me and all around me. I breathe in deeply and am filled with love and understanding".

SPIRITUAL MEANING

You have been gifted with the Great Spirit's energy of insight into future events. You feel that a situation is changing and your Soul is guiding you to step back and assess the situation before putting your full energy into it.

You are being guided to listen to your inner voice, that whisper you hear late at night that allows you to feel protected and at peace. Trust your instincts. You can't go wrong.

Affirmation: "I am so blessed in life and am so grateful of the life that I live. I am filled with Great Spirit's energy and the Universal signposts that I receive each day. My life path is clear of past hurts and I step forward into my future with peace and calmness".

HAWK FEATHER

PHYSICAL MEANING

You are being asked to listen to the advice that friends and family are giving you. The messages you are receiving about the decision you must make is correct and only comes from love. Allow yourself to let go of the control and surrender. You will always be guided to the best place for all involved. Allow your soul to be guided.

Affirmation: "I am so grateful for the love and guidance of my family and friends. I am so blessed that my life is filled with the company of loving souls and true friendships. My life is filled with honest communication and I am protected fully in that love".

SPIRITUAL MEANING

You are being asked to take notice of your dream state and waking state. The Universe, God, Spirit is delivering messages to you and you need to stop, breathe and take in those messages fully. Your life is taking a turn that will lead you on the path to happiness, joy, success and love. Stop. Listen. Write down your dreams. Listen to your messages.

Take notice of EVERY sign that is leaning you into a direction. You have the gift of hearing your past loved ones. Listen to them.

Affirmation: "I listen to my souls needs and am so grateful for my Universal gifts. I am so blessed that my life is filled with Universal protection. My life is incredible and I am gifted with insights that allow my life to be lived with happiness, joy and laughter".

COCKATOO FEATHER

PHYSICAL MEANING

Happiness and laughter surround you. You are being reminded not to take life so seriously. You are being asked to 'look out' for a health issue that is surrounding you. Your health needs close scrutiny and a cleansing needs to take place. A health check on adrenals and eyesight is needed.

You are being asked to 'look out' for a friend in need. Be aware of driving and where you are heading in the next week.

Affirmation: "I am so grateful that I am healthy and happy. My vision is clear and perfect and I am so blessed that my life is filled with happiness and laughter. I am protected. I am loved. I am guided".

SPIRITUAL MEANING

A gifting from a loved one that has passed. You are being told that you will always be 'looked after' and 'looked out' for. Protection on a high level. An insight to a friend's illness. A spiritual healing is needed.

A cleansing of the home, car and body, to bring forth a new protection and new direction in life.

Affirmation: "I love that I am protected by my (name of loved one). I feel their presence daily and that they walk beside me guiding me with love and laughter. I am so blessed that my life is filled with laughter and happiness and share my fortune with others so freely. The more love and laughter I give the more I receive".

CROW FEATHER

PHYSICAL MEANING

Magick is in the air. Your finances need to be closely looked at. Are you spending beyond your means? You are being guided to see the beauty in the magic of nature. Look towards nature for your answers. The energy of the full Moon will be the time to tell the Universe, God, Spirit of your goals. They WILL be achieved. Know this. This is your sign.

Affirmation: "I am filled with the energy of Moonlight. Each goal I have has succeeded, and in that success I give back more. I am so grateful that the magic of nature and the Universe guides me to financial freedom".

SPIRITUAL MEANING

A visitation from a male loved one that has passed. You are being asked to trust in the magick that surrounds you. This is in the form of financial freedom and a gifting of financial support. Accept this gifting fully, without hesitation. Be strong in your convictions when it comes to your dreams and goals. Affirm strongly that your goals HAVE succeeded and you are gifting the Universe your gratitude. This is what is needed to lift your energy, your soul to cleaner, clearer energy.

Affirmation: "I am surrounded by the magick of the Universe and accept the gifting that it gives me. My (name of loved one that has passed), guides me daily and I am so blessed to be in their presence. Money flows to me effortlessly. I am financially abundant. I am blessed with the insight of the Moon energy and believe in it's power. I am power-full in natures magick and am guided with grace".

OWL FEATHER

PHYSICAL MEANING

A healing is taking place. You are being asked to not stress so much over a situation to do with your house and home contents. Your home is protected, as is all the occupants. A new direction is needed, and the strength in your needs is linked with the pain in your knees and the pinched nerves in your neck. Look closely at the small print in contracts over the next month.

Affirmation: "I am so grateful that my family and home are fully protected. I am blessed that I see my future clearly. My financial success overflows into my personal and romantic relationships. I am one with the Universe and am filled with understanding and patience".

SPIRITUAL MEANING

A visitation from a female loved one that has passed. You are being asked to listen to your intuitive side. Your gut instinct is making you aware of a situation you need to keep a close eye on. Be aware of the 'push' to control a situation you have no control over. Acknowledge the energy of your loved one, and trust that they will guide you to the understanding and the space that you need to be in to make the correct decision for yourself and others' highest good.

Affirmation: "I am blessed with the Universal gifting of patience and understanding. I allow life to flow. My (name of loved one that has passed), guides me daily and I am so grateful to be in their presence. My intuition guides me and I allow the Universe, God, Spirit to move my life to a place of love, peace, calmness and connection".

WHITE FEATHER

PHYSICAL MEANING

You are being guided to express the truth in a situation that is around you. The outcome will favour those who are coming from a loving truth space, rather than a space of hurt. Breathe in the energy of compassion and peace, allowing all those involved to be surrounded by white feathered light. Know that you and all those involved are being guided to the best result. The truth will set you free. Believe and trust in this.

Affirmation: "I am expressing truth for the greatest good of all involved in this situation. I am so grateful that the best outcome was achieved. I honour myself with my words. I express myself with love. I am calm. My voice is strong. I express myself naturally. I am heard".

SPIRITUAL MEANING

A blessing is occurring. A cleansing is taking place by the highest order. You have wished for a cleansing of a situation and you have been heard. Breathe in the energy of acceptance, trust, compassion and be peace-filled. You are so loved, so adored by all those who have passed before you. Trust that you are being guided to start afresh. A blessing is occurring. A loved one that has passed is walking beside you, guiding you. Trust that you are in the right place for this healing to take place. You are being lifted up by Angels. You are strongly protected.

Affirmation: "I am blessed in every area of my life. I accept every Universal blessing with love and gratitude. I am grateful and receive blessings with an open heart and mind".

GREEN FEATHER

PHYSICAL MEANING

A healing is taking place. You are being told to listen to your instincts regarding your health and wellbeing.

You are being told to "lighten up". You may have been feeling low in energy and in need of a break and you are directed to do so now. Focusing on the food and drink you have consumed over the last few days, are you fuelling your body to the best of your ability? Are you consuming low energy/dense foods? (processed/packaged food). It is time to consume high energy fruits/vegetables/proteins. Choosing lighter foods allows your life and mood to 'lighten up'.

Affirmation: "I am the perfect weight for my height. I love being energetic and spontaneous. I trust that my body is being healed with the foods I consume".

SPIRITUAL MEANING

Your heart is being healed from a recent break of trust. You are being told that you are loved by those that have passed before you. They have felt your need for comfort, for healing, and they are assisting your soul to choose another path, another lighter outcome. Look for the signs, for they will be there. You are being wrapped up in the arms of Universal energy. It is time to trust again.

Affirmation: "I am open and ready to receive the best that life has to offer. I am so grateful for every blessing and love that I can give back more and more each day. I am excited about my new adventures!"

FLOURESCENT GREEN

PHYSICAL MEANING

Your money situation is about to change. An unexpected windfall. New adventures/new life. Fertility. A new life is being planned for you. You are being given a gift from the Universe. Accept positivity. Keep noticing the Universal signs around you. You are being led, you are being guided. Trust.

You are vibrating at the energy of wealth. You are being asked to accept a gift. Gratitude is surrounding you and you are in the right place at exactly the right time.

Affirmation: "I love that money follows me. I accept all forms of abundance in my life right now. I am free to do what I want and have what I need. My future is bright. I am financially free!"

SPIRITUAL MEANING

 A new life, new cells of healing forming. Choose light, happier, joyful energy to surround yourself with. You are being guided to let go of the past for good. Step into the future. Focus on happiness and health. A healing is taking place. Accept that the past is no longer relevant. Let go for good and let the Universe nurture you. Your guides are surrounding you with healing energy. They have been waiting.

Affirmation: "I am healthy, renewed and healed. My body and mind are happy and healthy. I choose happiness and health. With every breath I take I am becoming happier and healthier. I am happy. I am healthy. I am loved. I am healed".

TURQUOISE FEATHER

PHYSICAL MEANING

You are being asked to trust in a situation at work that is linked with your finances. A new promotion coming through. An unexpected advance in your finances. Laughter and fun. Water adventures. You may be asked to go on a trip across water. You are being guided to trust this new energy coming through, embrace it without fear. Your life path just got easier.

Affirmation: "I am so blessed and grateful for my life. My life is filled with adventure and laughter, happiness and joy. I am living a dream life and every day just gets better and better. I am so excited each day when I wake. My life is adventurous".

SPIRITUAL MEANING

Your Spiritual Guides are asking that you trust them. You are being directed to close a chapter on your life that no longer works for you. Stay strong during this change. Your life is about to take on a whole wonderful new adventure. A cleansing and clearing has taken place. Your dreams lead you to your new path. You are destined for success. It is time now to embrace that energy and let go of the fear of ridicule.

Affirmation: "I am now in exactly the right place in my life to succeed. Money flows to me easily and effortlessly. Every cell in my body vibrates success. I am financially and emotionally abundant. My life is filled with adventure and I embrace change freely. I am in tune with my higher self".

BLUE FEATHER

PHYSICAL MEANING

You are being guided to trust your own voice and speak up for yourself. A situation will present itself where you will have the opportunity to let another person know how you truly feel. Do not be scared or fearful of your own voice. Speak with love and with confidence. Know that your words have power. Give yourself a break and laugh more. See the funny side of life and express yourself with humour.

Affirmation: "I am grateful that I see the funny side of life. I love being quirky and my laughter fills a room and helps heal the planet. My voice is my best asset and I love that about myself".

SPIRITUAL MEANING

Your throat is healing from the harshness of the words you speak about yourself on a daily basis. It is time to give yourself a break and love yourself FIRST, then others. You have been so lost for so long you no longer trust yourself to speak. That time is now ending. Clear your throat, breathe in deeply and say what you need to say with heart and soul. Trust that the right words will come to you.

Your guides and the Universe are surrounding you with the energy of peace and acceptance. Allow your body to relax.

Affirmation: "I am so grateful that my words are loving and powerful. I love who I am and am grateful for the strength in my own voice. I say the best words at the best times".

ICE BLUE FEATHER

PHYSICAL MEANING

You are being asked to trust that you have been placed into a situation that needs your calm energy. You are being guided to clear the energy of miscommunication between friends and/or family. You are the peace maker. You know this. Now is the time to say what needs to be said and then walk away from the outcome. Allow peace to fill the situation and KNOW you have done all you need to do.

Affirmation: "I am the peace maker. I speak calmly and clearly in every situation that allows. I am heard, I am listened to. I allow myself to breathe in calm and speak calmly. I trust that my guidance places me in calm situations. I am loved and I am protected".

SPIRITUAL MEANING

You are a healer. You are so needed in this world for your calm thoughts and rationale. It is time to acknowledge this Universal gift for you have the gift of communication. Know that your words have power. They have the ability to heal. Trust that you speak from truth. You are the peacemaker. You are the channel. Using Blue Lace Agate will help you in your channelling abilities.

Affirmation: "I am a channel for truth. My words have power. I am grateful for the abilities I have and the strength of my words and voice. I acknowledge the Universal gifting inside of me. I trust my own power and speak calmly and truthfully".

RED FEATHER

PHYSICAL MEANING

A new romance is coming into your life. Rekindling of a current love, with renewed energy. Passion and purpose. Creativity and renovations. A tearing down of old energy replaced with new powerful energy. You have a drive to succeed. Successful outcomes to do with a situation concerning relationships and creative endeavours. A plan is forming. A favourable business dealing. Cupid's arrow. An old friend says goodbye.

Affirmation: "I am passionate. My life is full of purpose. I love my life. My life is filled with power and purpose. I am successful! I am loved and loving. I am loving and loved. Love surrounds me on a daily basis. I accept love wholeheartedly".

SPIRITUAL MEANING

Your energy is becoming stronger. You are vibrating with purpose and passion. Your guides are directing you to do what you love and your life will change for the better. Believe in your soul/life purpose.

A sexual repression is being let go of, to make way for a new self love. Allow your soul to heal and accept the Universal love that is showering upon you.

Affirmation: "I am filled with the love of the Universe. I trust myself. I am a great decision maker. I welcome and accept change. I am in a loving space with loving friends and family. I am loved fully".

PINK FEATHER

PHYSICAL MEANING

A loved one that has passed is sending you energy. Unconditional love of self and those around you. A pink Feather to Spirit is like that of a Red Rose. You are told you are loved. You are guided. You are surrounded by those who have passed before you. Trust that you are being guided and that you are on the right path. Breathe in love and breathe out all your stress. News of a new life forming.

Affirmation: "I am loved. I am guided. Every day is a reminder of the love that is shining down on me from Spirit. I move through life effortlessly. Life treats me beautifully and I am so grateful for all that I have. I am so blessed".

SPIRITUAL MEANING

You are being lifted up by Angelic forces. The depression and loneliness that you have been feeling is passing. Give that energy to Archangel Michael. Ask him to cut all ties with negative energy in your life. Bring into your life the energy of healing with Archangel Raphael. Allow the healing of unconditional love to change your entire life.

Affirmation: "I am so blessed and grateful for the love that I have in my life. I love who I am and who I have become. My life is filled with energy and vitality. I am filled with the energy of renewal and embrace the love that is flowing through me".

PURPLE/LILAC FEATHER

PHYSICAL MEANING

A physical healing is taking place. You may have noticed frequent headaches and a ring in your ears. This is part of the healing. Allow yourself to clear out the thoughts that are clouding your judgement. Know that this healing is very much needed to bring you into the alignment of your next step on your life path. Drink plenty of water. Get plenty of rest.

Affirmation: "I am so grateful for the healing that I am receiving. I am blessed that my body and mind are becoming balanced and I can think clearly and concisely. I am filled with the healing energy of the Universe and know that my life is blessed".

SPIRITUAL HEALING

A spiritual healing is taking place. The vibrational healing will lead you to high frequency in dreams and you may feel more migraines and pain behind the ears. Allow the healing to clear out any residual energy and know that you are being asked to trust the process. The Universe, God, Spirit has a plan for you which will come into fruition within 3 weeks. Watch for the Universal signs for they will be strong. Be aware of any past thoughts that do not belong in your future. Let go. Let God.

Affirmation: "I am healed with Universal energy. My body and mind are both balanced and aligned with my higher self. I am blessed beyond my wildest dreams. Everything I touch turns to Gold".

ORANGE FEATHER

PHYSICAL MEANING

A stirring of emotions. You are being told to listen to your instincts regarding a workplace situation. The flight or fight energy. Stomach upsets. You are being asked to trust in the Universe and let your ego step aside. Your emotions are getting the better of you. Hot tempers need to calm to resolve a situation. Freedom from an old flame.

Affirmation: "I trust that I am in the right place in my life. I am safe right now, right here. I am safe. I am protected. I trust my instincts. My instincts are correct. I am ok. I let go of the past and embrace the future. I believe I am safe".

SPIRITUAL MEANING

You have been given a life to live in service to others. Your guides, the Universe are acknowledging the energy you give to the World and sending it back to you to heal past hurts and heartache. You heart is healing and you are now able to move on past the hurt from others. A letting go to receive all that you need. Patience. Solitude. Standing firm in the face of adversity. Inner power and strength. Stability. Trusting your inner voice.

Affirmation: "I am guided. I am blessed. My life is filled with joy and I serve the Universe with the best of my ability. I love myself and my life. I am filled with love. I respect my body, mind and soul. I am in service to the Universe and am guided with love. I am all powerful and all loving".

YELLOW FEATHER

PHYSICAL MEANING

A new lighter life is happening. You have let go of the drudgery of the past and are embracing happiness and laughter. You are being guided to trust your instincts. Your 'gut health' needs to be checked. If you are having intestinal changes (eg: stomach upsets etc,.) this may indicate that something is not 'sitting well' with you. Trust your inner knowledge.

Affirmation: "I am filled with happiness and joy with each breath I take. Happiness follows me wherever I go. I see joy and happiness everywhere. I am nurtured and trust that I nurture my own body. I choose healthy, light, energised foods. Great health is attracted to me".

SPIRITUAL MEANING

You are being asked to cleanse your Solar Plexus Chakra - your intuitive chakra. Your intuition will become stronger as the Full Moon approaches and you will receive messages and intuitive guidance of where you need to be within the next few months. Your life is changing. A new outlook in life is coming. You are being guided to let go once and for all of the past and step onto the path of happiness. It is your time now.

Affirmation: "I embrace my intuitive side. My intuition leads me to fun, fulfilling loving spaces. I am an excellent judge of character. My inner glow shines forward and draws energy and happiness towards me. I embrace life with open arms. My life is filled with happiness and joy".

BROWN FEATHER

PHYSICAL MEANING

You are being asked to stop and contemplate which direction you would like your life to head. The direction of your life is being questioned, and you are being guided to stop, refocus, And THEN make a decision. A career change. Your life needs to be grounded. Clear your thoughts and allow the Universe, God, Spirit to lead you in the direction you need to go. Be aware of knee and joint pain in the next few weeks. The more severe the pain, the less directional certainty you are feeling.

Affirmation: "I am so grateful that my life is heading in the right direction. Every day I am on the path of personal success in body, mind and soul. I am so blessed with my clear path in life".

SPIRITUAL MEANING

You are being guided in a different direction in your life, and the Universe, God, Spirit is asking you to trust and have faith. The stress you are feeling is the lack of control you feel you have over a situation. Fear and stress are both illusions. Trust and Faith is what is needed in this situation. Walking near or in water is needed to cleanse the chakra of the feet and knees. Have faith that you will always be guided in the direction of the highest growth for your soul.

Affirmation: "I am so grateful that I am guided to a place in life where I am free of stress. I trust and have faith in myself daily. With every breath I take, and every step I make, my life gets better and better".

GREY FEATHER

PHYSICAL MEANING

A peace-filled energy is surrounding you. There is no need for you to do anything in a situation that you are currently in, as you are being surrounded by those that have passed and they are moving your energy to where it needs to be. Rest is needed. Allow yourself time out and know that you are loved. Tranquillity and calm energy surrounds you.

Affirmation: "I am so grateful that I am in a loving safe environment. I am blessed with a healthy body and a healthy mind. I am blessed with the love of my family and friends. My body resonates peace and calm".

SPIRITUAL MEANING

You are being guided to acknowledge the energy that you call towards you when you wake. A peace and calm is settling over you and you are being asked to trust that you and your family will all be safe and protected. A loved one that has passed is close by and you will feel a tug of your hair as an acknowledgement of this. Be still and know that you are loved, and that you are protected. Give permission for the loved one that has passed to visit you nightly in your dream state.

Affirmation: "I am so grateful that my dreams are filled with remembrances of love and laughter, happiness and joy. I am so blessed with the love of my family and friends. I give out love and receive love daily. I love who I am and where I am in my life. Life gifts me with love on a daily basis".

BLACK FEATHER

PHYSICAL MEANING

A healing is taking place. Your body has felt depleted of energy the last few days, and this gifting is to show you that your thoughts and prayers are being answered. Have faith and trust that you have been heard. A new adventure is on the horizon. You are being guided to let go of past hurts from an old friend. The energy of forgiveness is needed for you to move on. Forgive and let go. Allow the energy of healing to surround you. Breathe in new energy. Breathe out the past.

Affirmation: "I am surrounded each day with positive energy. Positive energy surrounds me and permeates from me. I give out good vibes and I get back good vibes. My body and mind are completely healed".

SPIRITUAL HEALING

You are being healed on every level of the body, mind and soul. Your energy is being heightened and a much needed healing has taken place. You are being asked to let go and let God, Universe, Spirit to lead you now where you need to be. You have done enough. It is time now for you to be looked after. Have faith that that is happening. Let go of the need to control life. Be at peace.

Affirmation: "I am filled with a peaceful energy. With every breath I take I trust and have faith in the Universe, God, Spirit. The Universe, God, Spirit guides me to the place of love and healing. I love my life and am so blessed and grateful for each and every day. I am alive with life and life is alive through me".

Chapter 7. Numero Uno - How the number of feathers can mean something unique.

I have always been fascinated with numbers. My old Maths teacher would laugh and laugh at that sentence. But, it's true. Numbers have such power. If we were to look at the Universe with a scientific mind through the eyes of a physicist, we would see the world in zero's and one's.

There is such power in numbers. I first came into girl crushin' on numbers when I read "The Life You Were Born To Live" by Dan Millman. And VOILA! The entire world made sense to me. My entire life and those around me made sense to me. I understood instantly that the numbers we were born into (our birthdate), holds the key to how and why we do things the way we do, and, most importantly, WHY we do, say and act the way we do.

So, I cannot write a book on The Meaning of Feathers without teaching you that the number of feathers that you have found/been gifted, is so very important. As important as the message that a Feather represents, so is the number you see appear.

And here you just thought a bird scratched and dropped a feather? Ha!

The following is a guide that will give you information on what energy the numbers 1 -9 mean as well as why they came to you in the first place.

The Number of Feathers:

One:

One represents an individual and one single situation. It is predominately classed as a strong sense of self, individualism and can at times depict a bit of a loner. The energy of a single Feather represents strength and a single personal message to the one who was gifted the Feather.

One also depicts that you need to take notice of the little things. A respect is earned and valued. It can also depict further study as the number is very mindful and studious.

Two:

Two represents communication and coupling. It is predominately classed as person who is works in the communication field and is very good with expressing their emotions. The energy of two feathers represents a spoken message and a relationship to the one who was gifted the Feather.

Two also depicts that you need to be aware of the words you choose. A relationship could be tainted if you are not aware of the value of your words and that which can hurt another.

Three:

Three represents the Trilogy. Mother Earth, Father Sky, Sister Moon. The Father, Son and Holy Ghost. The Physical, Mental and Emotional bodies. The Spiritual, Ethereal and Cosmic bodies. All in all it denotes grounding and looking towards a higher power or energy. It is predominately classed as a person who is looking for faith and finances, (don't those go hand in hand?) The faith in themselves and the path they are on, and the financial situation that they are in (having faith that money will come through when they need it etc,). The energy of three feathers represents a Spiritual Guide is making themselves known to the one who was gifted the Feather.

Three also depicts that you need to be aware of where you are putting your self-worth. Are you allowing 'things' to define you? Could there be a situation that you are spending your time on that could be spent somewhere else? Your money goes where your attention goes. Pay close attention to your financial affairs and the faith you are giving it.

Four:

Four represents stability and a strong foundation. It is predominately classed as a person who is grounded and can at times be too hard on themselves and those around them. A stickler for the rules. The energy of four feathers represents a need for grounding and rest to the one that was gifted the Feather.

Four also depicts that you need to remain true to yourself in the face of adversity. Choose your words carefully as your tone can be classed as harsh or unfeeling to those of a sensitive nature. Your body and mind need rest and recuperation. Just for one day do something you love, just because you love doing it. A masculine energy.

Five:

Five represents freedom from your own limitations. It is predominately classed as a person who is creative, yet can become anxious when life gets too chaotic. The energy of five feathers represents a need to acknowledge what part of their life they need to walk away from and what part they need to work on.

Five also depicts that you need to remember to breathe. You can run around too much and start too many projects without finishing them, and then become anxious when others begin to rely on you. Be aware of taking too much of life on at a time, and recognise that there are only so many things one person can do at one time. Try not to be so hard on yourself, and remember, there is so much perfection in being imperfect.

Six:

Six represents family and those friends you class as family. It is predominately classed as a person that is family orientated and has very much a high social conscience. The energy of six feathers represents a need to be cared for as much as you care for others. A love of self is needed.

Six also depicts that you need to fill your own cup of energy, and learn how to protect yourself spiritually from those around you who take your energy, leaving you lethargic and depleted. Look after your body. Drink in plenty of water. Chronic back pain tends to teach you how to rest, and give yourself time out. Be aware of where your energy is flowing, to how your life is going.

Seven:

Seven represents experience, personal, professional and experience of past mistakes. It is predominately classed as a person who is wise beyond their years, and is the opposite of the energy of a one, in the fact they do not like to be alone.

Seven also depicts that you need to recognise that just because you may feel lonely at times, you are never alone. Recognise the beauty and strength in 'alone time', and acknowledge that the need for personal freedom does not mean you need to push everyone away.

Eight:

Eight represents balance. Life balance as well as work balance. It is predominately classed as a person that needs a simpler kind of life, otherwise stress plays a major role in every area, causing an imbalance, and in extreme cases leading to co-dependence.

Eight also depicts that you need to re-focus your goals, wants and needs. Is there something you can let go of, so you can breathe easier? Is there a relationship that you feel pushed around in that you need to step away from? Your physical life needs to be balanced with a spiritual life. Reaffirm your faith, whether that be in the Universe, God, Spirit or just yourself.

Nine:

Nine represents completion. It is predominately classed as a person that needs to complete tasks before they start another, as well as someone that is relied upon by family and friends to clean up someone else's mess.

Nine also depicts that you need to stop dreaming, and get with the real world. Stand up for your own wants and needs, and try not to take on more than you can handle. Me first, then you, should be your motto. Let go that you will not be liked or loved if you stand up for yourself. Recognise your strength, in getting things done, completed, but also recognise your ability to walk away and not look back. The past may take a front seat in your life if you are feeling run down.

Ten:

Ten represents an individual's gift that they have brought through from a past life, and/or past life experience. It is predominately classed as a person that has the ability to see into future events and acknowledge where the energy is leaning towards.

Ten also depicts that you need to learn how to not push life too hard. Trust that you are being looked after yes, but try not to be so blasé that you are gifted the experience of hurt and pain over and over again until you learn the lesson fully. Be aware that you need to voice your emotional needs, and not feel others 'should' know how you feel.

Eleven:

Eleven represents psychic & clairvoyant abilities and experiences brought through from a past life, and/or past experience. It is predominately classed as a person that has the ability of empathy towards another's thoughts, feelings and needs. A tactile person, who may feel depleted in large crowds and become ill living in a hostile environment.

Eleven also depicts a Master Number. Read through number one's guide and acknowledge that the eleven represents double that energy. Double the positive energy as well as if you are living in a negative environment - you will be living in double the denser (negative) energy.

Chapter 8. Tune in and Tune out with Feathers:

If you are anything like me, you like to feel 'connected' to that which you hold dear.

The following is a technique I myself use to Tune in and Tune out to the Feather that has been gifted. The technique is as simple as can be, and all you really need is an open trustful heart, a clear mind and if you choose, a notepad and pen to write down the messages that you will receive from tuning in to your Feather.

Let's first TUNE IN to the Feather that has been gifted to us. You can either do this with eyes open or closed. I do both, to have the best of the best worlds of sight, touch and feel.

The number one thing to be sure of is to hold the Feather in the hand you received it in. For example, when first seeing the Feather did you see it on your Right (Physical) side, or Left (Spiritual) side.

TUNE IN TECHNIQUE

Close your eyes (if you are choosing this method) and use your sense of feel and touch. If you have your eyes opened, be sure to use ALL your senses (sight, touch etc,.) equally.

1. How does the Feather feel in your hand?
   Heavy or Light?

2. Do you want to hold the Feather you are holding
   Closer to you?
   Away from you?
   Neutral distance?

3. Are you pointing the tip of the Feather
   Away from you?
   Towards you?
   Facing Right?
   Facing Left?

4. Using your sense of touch and feel, does the Feather feel
   Rough?
   Smooth?
   Jagged?
   Missing pieces?

Now after noticing what you answered above, look through the guide below to gain more insight in to your Feathers' message for you:

Feather feels heavy:

You are being asked to allow the Universe, God, Spirit to take your burdens and stress from you. There is such strength in vulnerability and the Universe, God, Spirit is guiding you to a place of acknowledging the strength in asking for help. Ask and yee shall receive.

Feather feels light:

The Universe, God, Spirit is rewarding you with a burst of healing energy of pure love, pure light. This healing is for your entire body, mind and soul to be lifted towards the abundance of all that light has to offer you. Embrace this lightness. Take the energy of light within and allow it to shine out to others.

Wanting to hold it closer:

You are feeling the 'pull' energy of the messages you are receiving with the gifting of this Feather. It is time to change your life, and you are in exactly the right space and the right time to do this. Write out all the messages this Feather represents and acknowledge that your soul is urging you to take action. Your life is filling with adventure. Are you ready?

Wanting to hold it away:

The 'fight or flight' and 'push' energies are very strong with you, and you are being asked just to relax and allow the Universe, God, Spirit to guide you. There is no need to control your life, as your life works wonders when it is allowed to express itself with spontaneity. Allow the Universe, God, Spirit to create miracles in your life. You will be glad that you did.

Wanting to hold it at neutral distance:

You are weighing up the outcome before you invest your energy and emotions. You may feel unsure in life and wanting others to take control so you do not hurt another's feelings with your actions. It is time to take action, for your life, for your happiness, for your future. This is the perfect time for you. Allow the Universe, God, Spirit to guide you. You will never be in harm's way as you are always protected. THIS is your soul's journey. Allow your body to go along for the ride and put your need to over-think it to rest. Be still and become free.

Pointing the Feather away from you:

You are being asked to notice the energy that you are giving to others. Are you giving all your power away? Do you feel that if you give more you are loved more? Notice the answer that you came up with and know that no matter what you do, how you act, you will always be loved fully by the Universe, God, Spirit. Let the energy of life fill you.

Pointing the Feather towards you:

You are powerful in your knowledge that this gifting is for you and you alone. Take the messages that you have been given and allow them to work with you, to lift you higher in the knowledge that you are always protected, loved and guided. There is never a better time than now to give yourself the gifting of remembrance. Know that you and the Universe, God, Spirit are ONE.

Facing right:

Your physical needs are outweighing your spiritual needs. Find the balance in life and your life will be balanced. Allow the messages to guide you to a place where you are free to let go of the past and embrace the future with positivity and lightness of spirit.

Facing left:

Your spiritual needs are overshadowing your physical needs. This can be in the form of an illness that you have carried through space and time (lifetimes). Allow the messages you are being gifted to heal you of the past once and for all and embrace this life with love, strength, renewal, laughter and a healed soul. You have done enough. It is time to shine.

Does it feel rough?

You are being asked to 'take the edge off' your thoughts, words and actions. You speak so harshly about yourself that your body is creating illness and suffering. Let go of the anger you have of the past and embrace healing, health and happiness. Allow life to be and feel smoother.

Does it feel smooth?

You may have been feeling highly emotional and teary lately. This is ok. It is ok to feel emotion. As long as when you do feel that emotion you allow the energy it's time and then let it go. Try not to get caught up in 'holding on' too tightly to any emotion that happens. Your life will become balanced once you find the ebb and flow energy. Allow that to come, like a breeze in the trees, or an ocean wave. Breathe in that energy. Allow it to become one with you.

Does it feel jagged?

Your energy levels are not balancing while you sleep. Have you changed your sleeping arrangements lately? Your night time routine needs reassessing. You need healing on both the physical and spiritual levels. A situation in your life has 'knocked you off kilter' and you may be feeling your life is spinning out of control. Once a healing has been done, your life will become more centred, more balanced. Allow the Universe, God, Spirit to guide you to the place of healing. It is much needed at this time.

Does it feel like it has pieces missing?

Is there a certain time in your life you can think of right at this moment when someone hurt you so badly you felt like they tore a piece of your soul? This Feather gifting is for that piece to know how to heal and for you to step into a brighter, happier, healthier future. You paid your Karmic debt. Allow the Universe, God, Spirit to clean the slate. You can start again.

TUNE OUT TECHNIQUE

I use this technique to allow myself to go further into the experience of the gifting of the Feather and really delve deep into the Universe, God, Spirit's message.

By visualising a Spiritual Guide, a Loved one that has passed, or the bird that the Feather originally came from, I then am gifted with the most incredible messages. But not only that, I am gifted with the remembrance that I am never alone, that I am ALWAYS guided, and that I am connected to all things, everywhere. ALL IS ONE, IS ONE.

To do this technique all you need to do is to be seated or lying down in a comfortable position and lay the feather on your chest or stomach with the tip of the feather pointing towards your head and the stem (end) of the feather to be pointing to your toes.

I prefer to do this technique in silence, but if you choose to, you can use music of your choice that allows you to feel calm, peace and allows you to shut out all outside noises and influences.

The technique:

1. Breathe in and out deeply 5 times, allow your chest to rise and fall until your breathing is comfortably spaced. This is the time to move around a bit to make sure you are completely comfortable.

2. Taking a deep breath in, visualise the Feather rising and falling. The deeper the breath in, the higher the Feather rises, the longer you breathe out, the slower the Feather floats towards you. Do this for 10 breaths.

3. Continue breathing deeper and slower and visualise the colour of the Feather. Is it the same colour as the one that you placed on your chest? Take notice of the colour (if it has changed) and see that it is rising higher and higher with each breath in, and each breath out.

4. The Feather now is floating higher and higher above you. Notice how you are feeling. Feel the emotions and then allow them to float away, slow and steady, just like the Feather is rising higher and higher but still within sight.

5. Ask now for your Loved one, Spiritual Guide, Messenger to come forward and sit beside you. Allow them to heal you, to speak to you, to listen to you, to be in your energy with you. Stay in this moment for as long as you need. If you feel twinges in your body, notice them, and then allow them to float away. This is your time to receive all that you need from the Universe, God, Spirit.

6. When you feel the time is right, thank your Loved one, Spiritual Guide, Messenger and embrace your energy with theirs. Connect with them fully and see that you and they are ONE. Breathe in the knowledge that you can call on each other whenever you need too.

7. Breathe in deeply and slowly and release your breath slow and steady, noticing the Feather returning slowly, floating down

towards you, with each breath in and comes closer and, with each breath out it floats nearer, until it is resting back where you placed it.

8. Sit/lie in this energy for as long as you need to, slowly becoming aware of your surroundings. Wiggle your toes slowly and your fingers. Relax in this peace-filled state for as long as you need to. Gift yourself this time to just BE.

When you are ready, write down in your notepad/journal the experience of your TUNE OUT technique with that particular Feather. Did you receive any new information? Was it a loved one that has passed that came to visit? Did you see colour? Smell different scents? Have a physical sensation happen?

You can do this technique as many times as you would like.

It is such a powerful and beautiful way to connect with life, the Universe, God, Spirit.

May you always feel that connection.

May your life be filled with memories of light, happiness, joy, success and love and may those memories last you lifetimes.

Love & Squishy hugs.

Nicole

July, 2014

Have you loved this book?

I would love to hear from you!

Come say Hi at

http://spiritualwisdommagazine.com

Join me and others at
http://facebook.com/spiritualwisdompublishing

http://facebook.com/nicolesuzannebrownauthor

AND

Become an ARC Angel!
https://www.facebook.com/groups/NicolesARCAngels/

Write a review on Amazon & Goodreads to share with others what you loved.

Chapter 9. About Nicole:

Nicole Suzanne Brown lived in sunny Queensland all her life until moving to a very small cold country town of New South Wales, and still is confused by the choice to this day. Small in stature but big in personality, she has lived in New York, the United Kingdom, spent time in an Indian Ashram and gets itchy feet every time she glances at her Passport.

She is the Creator and Editor of Spiritual Wisdom Magazine an online publishing resource for spiritual authors and bloggers.

She is the Author of Passing through Time – conversations with the other side, The Creativity Workbook, The Wee Little Book of The Awesome, Give to Get - how to give to receive all that you need and the soon to be released Fictions: Pride, Outback Mistress, and Phoenix.

When not writing you can find her contemplating her navel, somewhere, in some part of the world.

Other works by Nicole Suzanne Brown

> ### Passing through Time
> ### (conversations with the other side)

Jason was a strong, fit and healthy young man with everything to look forward to in life.

His death of a heart attack at 29 years of age was a sudden shock to his loved ones. It was a short time later that he started to communicate with his sister Nicole. Jason explains to his sister what he saw when he died, or as he calls it "Passing through Time". Jason describes the feelings of overwhelming peace and love that you experience when you pass through time, as well as what others experience (children, car accident victims, etc,.)Jason also speaks about how we can naturally heal the human body through positive affirmation and meditation, Angels, Forgiveness, the energy of God, and the energy of pure Love that is available to us all.

"Passing Through Time is 'conversations with God' on a more intimate, realistic scale.

A lot of questions one might pose to God, or what we as mortal humans have perhaps considered inwardly, quietly to ourselves, Nicole openly asks her brother Jason, who has passed away in the prime of his life.

He tells Nicole his own personal spiritual life experiences from 'the other side'. Nicole shows no fear in communicating with Jason, I would be a little uncomfortable in the same situation. However, she is perfectly comfortable sensing Jason's presence.

I love that Jason indicates to Nicole that life is the 'illusion', and death a kind of 'reality'. Regardless whether or not you believe in life after death, it's an interesting take on the philosophy of life.

Nicole cleverly interspersed the stark reality of Jason's sudden death via short takes from her Mum's diary. A humbling reminder of the other side of death, that whilst Jason is happy and content, those left behind are struggling. An enlightening read. Comforting and reassuring, no matter which side of the fence you sit on regarding your own personal beliefs on the big question, does life after death exist?"

Aishah Macgill,
co-founder of Australian Writers Rock

"Nicole Brown's book – "Passing through Time" is a beautiful breath of fresh Energy. It encapsulates Spiritual Philosophy and Spiritual Truths succinctly, and in such a way that really guides the reader through what may otherwise be very esoteric information. It was like re-connecting with a very wise friend. A Must-Read for anyone wanting to understand the Spiritual Dimensions of Life – this One and the Next!"

Donna Nelson
www.TheSpiritualAdventuresOf.com

"Passing through Time" written by Nicole Suzanne Brown is compelling, for anyone who has lost a loved one this throws light on a sensitive subject of death and yet Nicole's experience and illuminated interpretation gives great comfort for those who have had loved ones pass over. Not only does Nicole show a great depth of insight into the other dimensions that surround us in a new and inspired way this book is a rare find and a must read for anyone serious about their spiritual evolvement.

Jan-Marie Brooke
www.inspiredbrilliance.com.au

Chapter one of Passing Through Time - Conversations with the Other Side
Introduction

Jason was strong, fit and healthy. His death at age 29 of a heart attack on 20th December, 1998, came as a sudden shock to myself, my parents and his fiancé Gaylene (just engaged the day he died).

Through remembrance of his love for us all and mine for him, we began speaking to each other shortly after his death.

The following conversations of his adventures and remembrances of passing through time gave us all great comfort and helped us live through our loss and sadness. He continues to communicate with me, and has taught me about what it is like to die, or as he chooses to call it 'Pass through Time'. Revelations of love, truth and peace-filled existence of the after-life is evident in his learning's and memories.

His and my only wish is for all of us not to fear 'death' or have fears for the loved ones that have passed 'before' us, but to remember and reconnect with each other through the love we share.

Nicole 2012

'I'm so happy now Mum.

I've found my purpose'

Jason 16/12/98

First Conversation with Jason

The feelings of grief cannot be explained in layman's terms. For every single person it is an individual experience.

Some get angry, others remorseful. But, the most important thing for anyone, everyone, is that they feel every feeling to its full extent.

The first conversation I had with Jay was only days after he passed. Days for us, a lifetime for him. I was lying on his bed, listening to his favorite song, consumed with grief, confusion, heartbroken and lonely. I kept asking why? Why him, why now? When there were so many nasty people in the world, why 'take' him? I questioned GOD. I questioned every belief I had. And in that questioning with my own thoughts raging in my head, I heard him.

I will never publish the first conversation that we had. It was deeply personal. Messages for family and friends, loving memories that he had for each of us and only us. But in that first conversation we connected through time, through energy and through the love we have for each other.

It's so important to be connected right now with the ones you love. Tell them how deeply you feel; tell them how grateful you are that they are who they are. Let them know that no matter what happens, not matter where you are in the world you *will* connect. Oceans apart or eons apart. You will always be connected.

Our family did that in the last phone call we had with Jay only hours before he passed.

We kept our promise.

We now hope we can teach you to make and keep yours.

Nicole 2012.

My Son is dead.

My heart is breaking and my

Son is dead.

Journal entry – 21/12/98

Mum

Jason's Experience

Jay, what did dying feel like? So many people are so terrified of death. And I think it's the 'not knowing' that scares the crap out of everyone, even the most resilient.

For me personally, because everyone's experience of passing is different 'as is their life, so is their death' it was the most peaceful thing I have ever felt.

I remember laughing with Gaylene and making plans for our wedding and also our future. I remember lying there and talking with her with the lights out and I held her hand when I was falling asleep.

Then I remembered that I had this feeling of total peacefulness, it was like I was finally complete. I was grateful for all that struggle in my life to get me right here to this place right now. I knew where I was going in life, who I was, where I finally fitted in. I guess I had never really done that before - given thanks, been grateful, truly grateful for all that I have and don't have. I was grateful for the woman lying next to me, for Mum, Dad and you. My friends; for all that I received and had, I 'knew' who I was, finally. It's like I got it! I found the last piece of the puzzle, the clue to the riddle. I worked out the meaning of life.
I remember saying 'If this is the happiest I am ever going to be'...
Then ...

… I was outside of myself, looking over Gaylene and I sleeping. I was lying on my stomach with my leg off to one side. There were all these colors around me. At first I thought they were all around me and then I noticed the colors were around everything.

It's amazing Nicole. Every time I breathed in, the colours changed to brighter vibrant colors. Then every time I breathed out, they become pastel colors, still vibrant but not as bright. I remember lifting my hand up and watching the gold light like a wave, going not only around my hand, but through it as well. When I breathed in, things like objects became denser and when I breathed back out, they were shimmery, like a wave, like heat on a road. I guess that's how they explain energy. I remembered thinking this is what astral travelling is probably like.

I remember looking around the room and 'pushing' the colors with my hands. The colors moved and glided. They didn't crash into each other or become jagged or fragmented. They danced and gelled into each other, separating and then coming back together again. I'd never seen anything like it on Earth, but I just knew it was right. I wasn't scared or nervous I was excited and knew that that's how life was, always. That's how it is and we just don't see it.

I then looked more closely at my face.
I remember thinking and feeling that it looked so grey and old, when all I felt was really young and fit. I guess you could say it was that I felt alive for the first time in my life. Really alive. Free. When I was looking at myself, it all began to change.

I realized when I breathed in I could see everything inside me, my lungs and my bones, my skeleton and my heart. I looked over at Gaylene and could see the same thing, her lungs going in and out with every breath she took and her heart beating. I smiled at her 'cause she looked so beautiful and peaceful. I looked back at myself again, lying there beside her and noticed something was different.

It took me a while I guess, looking back and forth from myself to Gaylene when it dawned on me. My lungs weren't moving and my heart wasn't beating like hers. It wasn't beating at all. When I realized what that meant, I thought for a second that I should feel scared. I tried to and waited for the panic and fear to rise inside me...but it never came. I sat there for what seemed a long time, just looking at myself. Looking at my body, my face …

… And then I began to cry. Not because I was sad or scared, but because I wasn't. I knew what it all meant. I had died. It was sudden and not at all like I thought I would die. But I knew that I had left time behind for the last time. I was free. I didn't feel sad or frustrated or worthless. I didn't feel that struggle or fight to be good or funny or liked. I didn't feel anything negative at all. Just peaceful. Only peace.

After a while of sitting there, I wiped the tears from my eyes and looked down at them on my hands. My tears had now become gold light and energy. I remember thinking 'so that's what pure love looks like'.

I looked up and all the colors around me had become really bright and vibrated. Then through the colors came these people, or Beings of Light I suppose you would call them. And they were smiling at me. I remember looking at the Beings and shrugged my shoulders at them. Not like a 'well, what's next?' thing, but a 'So, this is it' thing.

They nodded as if they knew what I was thinking, and then they smiled at me and came closer.

It's funny to remember it now, but when you look at these Beings, their appearance changes to whatever or whoever you think about. The first thing I thought of was 'will I see Charlie Brown?' - our childhood dog. Isn't that funny? Then suddenly there he was, this being changed instantly into Charlie and came bounding up to me. I laughed and cried as I held him cause he was exactly how I remembered him.
I then thought of White Feather - my spirit guide and another Being changed into him instantly. He was a lot taller than I thought he would be and I guess the surprised look on my face is what made him laugh. As soon as we touched all the memories we had shared together over our lifetimes with him came flooding back, especially the times in this life, when I thought I had no-one, I could see now that he was there, standing behind me with his hand on my shoulder like he was just then.

I then thought of your spirit guide Nicole - Soaring Eagle and White Feather instantly changed his appearance to look like your guide, or how I imagined him to look - I'll talk to you more about that later. I thought of Mum's guide and again the face and the body of the Being changed. I must have thought something because I suddenly heard in my head that 'WE ARE ALL ONE - ALL PART OF EACH OTHER'

I thought of Grandad and Uncle Terry and Aunty Gloria and these Beings came through the colors and changed into them.

We all laughed and hugged each other. Uncle Terry looked really healthy, really young like I remembered him when we used to go fishing, or over at his place where we played pool. I must have started thinking of a lot of people then, because more and more Beings changed appearance to look like who I was thinking of. I even thought of Peter Allen - the singer - I don't know why; and he came in front of me. Now, HE'S a lot shorter than I thought he would be (laughs).
I then thought of you, Mum and Dad and looked back around to see myself lying there again. Beings changed into you, Mum and Dad and everyone I thought of that wasn't dead.

For a split second, I couldn't understand why.

There is No Time

Then as soon as I thought about it the answer came. 'There is no time'. Our lives truly are instant Nicole. What we see as a 'lifetime' really is just a blink of an eye or a single breath.

You and Mum and Dad and I all hugged and the memories of our lives together came flooding back, things I thought I had forgotten were instantly relived and we laughed and cried and I was once again thankful for having the life I had shared with you all.

I looked over at Gaylene and she began to wake up. I was concerned for her, although that 'feeling' didn't come over me - just the thought. I heard her telling me to roll over because she thought I was snoring. She then touched me and I saw my body go all stiff like an ironing board. It was like all my muscles went into spasm. She then jumped out of bed, ran over to turn on the light, and then was at my side rolling me over. She stepped back for a moment because my eyes were wide open. Then she put her head to my chest, checked if I was breathing and started CPR.

Gaylene ran out of the room and called for an ambulance running back to check on me again and again trying CPR waiting for the ambulance to come. It was a strange feeling standing there viewing it all, watching her fight for my life. I thought that I would feel a pull emotionally or frightened or scared, but none of those feelings came. Then I realized something, and in that realization I turned next to me and a Being changed into Gaylene. She was with me, the energy of her, the energy of all that I loved about her was right here with me, witnessing it all with me, being there again for me. I thanked her for fighting for my life. I thanked her for loving me in my life, I thanked her for the person she was and thanked her for the memories I will always share and have with her.

Even though all of this was only just happening it was like it happened a long time ago, like when you stub your toe, or hit your thumb with a hammer. You remember it hurt, but that's all, you just remember. The pain doesn't come with those memories; you just remember that back then, it hurt.

I don't want to dwell too much on my passing. I would rather, am here to, help you write, to remember with me, to learn and teach others about a more realistic experience of life on earth and on death, or as we like to call it 'Passing through Time'. Passing through time Nicole is an adventure, a mystery, an answer to the unknown that Western civilization (myself included), search for all their lives.

It is a plausible realization of the GOD-Force, GOD-Self in all of us. It is energy. It is pure love.
It is a fantastic area of life that we have closed the door on for so long; we forgot the great adventure it holds.

The realization of the Human Spirit is upon us. In your lifetime you will grasp your dreams, live your dreams in reality.

That is all we want, isn't it? Hopefully with these writings, people will begin to not search for the meaning of life but instead live and 'Be' their answer, only striving for them 'selves' the essence of who they really are.

I will tell you of great things, unbelievable sights and realizations as I come upon them and them upon me.
This is my calling I have found my way.

Allow me to teach you to find yours.

Jason.

Jay, several times throughout these communications you have stated that 'when you take your first breath when you pass'. Does that mean you breathe after death? (I hear Jay breathe in and out and then 'feel' his shoulders shrug).

Yeah, I guess so. I never really thought about it. But then again, how many times on Earth do you actually 'think' about breathing. Remember, life is the illusion. Passing through time is the reality.
Can you feel?

Absolutely! The feelings are intensified to such a rapid vibration that all you do is feel. As I just explained, when communicating here and with you, feeling is everything. There is nothing separate or apart from that essence of energy.

I feel such love, more than I ever felt capable of or knew even existed. I feel peace, joy, excitement, anticipation, love for you all and also love for myself. Some here do feel anger or bitterness, but once they realize the energy that surrounds them, is them, they move rapidly into the energy of peace and love, that is just the energy of learning and remembrance.

Do you have a body that you are aware of?

When you pass, initially you have the 'thought' of the body that you did when you were on earth because it is comfortable and familiar.

Then when you become accustomed and used to the energy around you, you notice a change in your physical self. You become lighter and less dense in your energy. You become more luminescent with your surroundings. You can call energy into your being until you realize that that's just what you are already - intellectual energy.

You begin to vibrate at a more rapid vibrational structure than you ever could on Earth. Therefore there is no need for such a dense vibrational form as a 'physical' body.

I can still be in the form of 'Jason' whenever I want or choose to be. The energy vibration of that intellect is just remembering or oscillating at a more defined or higher vibration molecularly. I like this form and these memories. I suppose you can say I'm just a mere shadow of my former self (laughs).

When I speak to you I am able to remember or re-invent the molecular structure of 'Jason' because you are used to that energy. You are comfortable with it. You are accustomed to it. You are also, importantly, connected to that particular vision of the energy I oscillate with. Now, by using the energy and becoming one with it, I am able, if I feel like it, to transcend my energy to an energy level outside of the physical form. We all do it, here and where you are. Although you call it 'dream state/astral travel'. Same thing. Now, when we greet people who have passed and say their individual Prayer of Remembrance, we come in light form or 'light bodies'- bodies of light. That's what I saw when I passed and now I am one of them when other's pass. It seems to help the person passing through to 'remember' who they are and why they are.

The light that we emit is a remembrance and a resurgence of peace-filled love moving at a slightly higher vibration to that of Earth. You're kind of eased into the realization of remembrance. The energy then moves them to a particular energy- based realized form. We are all part of ourselves.

Have you any depth of the physical? Can you touch, smell etc?

Again, of course. Remember, the physical is the illusion. There on Earth, we use only 12% of our brain or intellect (some even less - laughs). The only reason that humans have the 'lower' intellect of remembrance is just that; they have forgotten their remembrance of the intellect.

Once humans establish a re-connection with their own vibration, their intellect then grows or oscillates at a higher more rapid energy. You are able to access more because, in remembrance, your intellect opens more to new ideas and growth 'spurts'. I am able to touch, smell, hear and see etc,. as I did on Earth, but again, at a more rapid molecular structure. I can also touch, hear, smell and see you in your own molecular structure. The touch you receive feels sometimes like a feather has brushed your face or hands.

Depending on the energy you are oscillating at, at a particular time, the touch may become stronger. Being in touch with your loved ones, connecting so strongly through thought, feeling, love and remembrance allows the boundaries to be lifted and the energy to flow freely. Your energy connecting with mine is through the energy of remembrance so you are able to 'receive' more senses. In those circumstances, the touch will become more direct - like someone poking you in the eye, sticking their finger in your ear, pulling your hair, or taps on the shoulder etc,.

It is in the energy of connection of remembrance that allows us all to communicate with each other, everywhere. Heaven literally on Earth. Hopefully with our conversations, the people will begin to open their collective thoughts just enough to allow that to happen. More people especially in the western world seeking communication openly and lovingly will allow energy to move and evolve. Conflicts will lessen and love will shine through. Learning's of spirituality will be honored and taught from cradle to grave. Openly without fear, without boundaries. Eastern teachings know this, yet the western world is still lost, still confused, still feels alone and isolated.

Passing Through Time - Conversations with the Other Side available through <u>Amazon</u>, <u>Kindle</u> & Nicole's bookshop <u>spiritualwisdommagazine.com/ebooks</u> <u>spiritualwisdommagazine.com/signed-paperback</u>

Fiction novels also by Nicole Suzanne Brown

Outback Mistress (out Dec, 2014)

"A wayward sister returns to her homestead, only to find her brother, a highly decorated Police Officer murdered, and the entire town acting suspiciously.".

CHAPTER 1.

Living in a small Country town is not for the faint hearted. Even though Portland is not your typical town, there isn't the growing space for mediocrity. You either fit in or move out. It's that simple. With its tiny butter box houses, littered out front with planter boxes of pansies and lavender, neighbours who have been friends since kindergarten sit on their front porch swings, lazily waving their hands across their faces to shoo away the sticky flies, gossip over the latest rumour and chastise their children all in one sentence. Feuds between families last generations in this town even though no one knows why or how it started in the first place. Honour is placed highly. Honour and survival. Weatherboard sheds tuck behind each house, paint split and curling in the harsh heat and bitterly cold winters. Wind willies dance along dirt laid laneways kicking up red dust, scattering across the yards, settling on the early morning washing. Kookaburra's laughter mingles with the sounds of distant children playing against the breeze while bees gather pollen around their feet. With the Queensland floods the then drought stricken land, revived, now lush, the grass so green it hurts your eyes. The population almost halved years ago when the old cement mill shut down. Now those that stubbornly stayed, daring to see the tough times out, are firmly planted like that of the swaying willow down by Portland's creek beds.

This town was once abundant. It was incredibly affluent in every sense of the word. It was a town of wealth and business, prestige and money. It was a town of productivity and employment. It was the town that built Sydney. Those skyscrapers you see, work in, dance around to avoid the traffic in that huge Metropolitan, the townsfolk of Portland made those for you. Sydney was built with Portland cement. Its Earth is in every cell. The town of Portland is in its D.N.A. It breathes because of this town. It grows now because of Portland's foundation.

It is a strong town. A proud town. Full of strong personalities and an ever beating heart. When the Cement works closed it felt like the breath was sucked out too. The riches and abundance left the town. Only the strong survived. Those that remembered. Those that never gave up hope that one day the town would turn around, but after a decade the town now is now lost, counting on one hand the businesses that have stayed open and struggle each week to do so.

Nothing much happens here. The odd domestic disturbance when the welfare cheque runs out and the alcohol dares to run low. A few drunken disorderly misdemeanors when one of the young men turn 18, many more when an old farmer dies from self inflicted injuries. With one grocery store, connected to the pub, a school that hosts kindergarten to high school, and a large graveyard on the outskirts of town, several large cattle properties nestle amongst the hills, there wasn't much that Matthew Noble couldn't keep an eye on. He runs his hands through his short cropped hair; adjusts his gun belt on his hip and leans back against the bar.

The pub was busy, and Matthew Noble was happy that they were all in one place at the one time so he could keep an eye on them. Having returned back to the homestead a fully decorated police officer years before, he loved the quiet paced energy of the town compared to the rat race of Sydney. The generosity and individuality of the town folk that jostle and laugh around him excited to be spending his Birthday welcomed him back to the fold; more so now that he shouted the last two rounds. He was, in the eyes of the small community, a top bloke. He watches the clock that hangs precariously above the fireplace and counts down the seconds till it chimes eleven times. He figured an hour out of his night shift was enough to be seen as being seen, but he needed to also make a quiet exit so he didn't cramp anyone's style, let alone his own.

Marv Grainer lazily leans against the bar allowing his beer gut to hang on the lower shelf. A huge man with small stature, he kept the alcohol flowing and the bar tabs to a minimum. He had inherited the bar from his father and his before him. Late at night when the bar is empty and the drunkards have all staggered home, he fires up sing star opera and dreams of a time when he could have done whatever he wanted with his life. Yet he knew dreams and wishes are for fools and you have to work with what you've been given. He catches a glimpse of Matthew heading towards the exit and bellows over the conversations of the patrons. "Matt! Come on mate! My shout this time..!" Matthew waves his hand no, following with a thumbs up sign and steps out to the cold night air. "Piker" Marv grunts pushing back a young cowhand shaking his empty schooner glass in his face "Not you, ya fucknut"

The night air's crisp clean smell is quickly replaced by the harsh green coal smoke that lingers above all the houses around town. The town is frugal with their money with no sense or compassion for environmental damage their warm houses cause. Matthew sniffs and clears his throat, shrugging his coat up closely to cover his neck. He strides over to his patrol car, pulling his key out of his pocket.

Lisa Muller stands on the balcony eyeing Matthew with interest. Dressed in low cut second-hand lingerie, she is a tiny girl, with straight blonde hair down to her waist, a bubbly personality and the town's jezebel. Of course ask any man in this town and they will emphatically deny it. The women, however, will not. She leans over the rail and purrs sweet and low "Happy Birthday Handsome" Matthew stops short turning to look up. He has known her since grade school, was her first kiss, and knew she had a sweet spot for him, as he did her, but never really grew too attached to her. He never really grew too attached to anyone, except for his homestead and the land that surrounds it. He touches the brim of his Police baseball cap and smiles shyly "Thank you Lisa, I appreciate that". She smiles big and nods back towards her bedroom "Don't feel like coming in for a little celebration do you?" He shakes his head and smiles up at her causing her heart to do a double beat while her stomach flip flops. He shakes his head no "I'm all partied out, but thank you tho". Lisa pouts playfully "Oh, I'm sure we can find something else to do to keep each other entertained" Matthew looks down and scuffs his shoe against the dirt plastered on his front tyre. "I'm sure we could Lisa. Maybe some other time. Thank you again tho. You have a good night. Keep safe now". Lisa swoons "Matthew, you are such a polite, sweet thing, someone's going to take advantage of that someday. Maybe even me" Matthew laughs up at her "Maybe Lisa. Night."

She watches his strong shoulders and tight arse get into the car and wishes her life was so very much different to what she was living right now. She closes her eyes, momentarily drowning out the snoring patron sprawled on her bed behind her, clothes and a gun belt strewn over her lounge and floor and dreams of simpler, happier times.

Justin, a pimpled skin, skinny man poking his head out of the front door of the pub yells up at her, breaking her out of her daydream "Hey Lisa! Why don't we do something different tonight and you pay me?" Lisa's good mood vanishes like coal smoke on a winter's breeze, She flinches, shows him her middle finger and steps back through her glittered nylon curtains, back to the daydream, far away from here. Justin is jostled back to the bar, his voice gruff "What is it with that woman, with men in uniform?" he slumps at the bar and taps his glass for a refill "I'm sure a lot of women would find sanitation worker's uniforms attractive mate" Marv slides the beer over to him, stopping expertly in front of the saddened sanitary worker. He sulks into his beer "They only want you if something's stuck-up or needs plunging" Marv snorts, "You should be more popular then mate!"

Matthew, hands on hips, stands on the side of a dirt road on the outskirts of town, staring down at his back tyre now flat and shredded to the rim. For the last half hour he has driven slowly through the town streets and past properties making sure all those who are not still at the pub are tucked tightly and safely in their homes. He kicks the tyre with his foot, takes his cap off, scratches the back of his head, walks around to the back of the car popping the boot, pulling out the tyre jack and spare tyre. He plonks himself down on the spare tyre and goes to work loosening the wheel nuts.

A Ute slowly drives towards Matthew, tyres scrunching over the dry dirt road stopping short just meters away, high beams piercing through the darkness. The driver jumps down from the car. Matthew squints, shielding his eyes from the glare of the lights. He instantly recognises the driver approaching. He leans back on his heels and points at his tyre. "Well hello stranger, long time no see. Can you believe my luck? Tonight of all nights." He turns back to loosen the last wing nut "What you doing out this way?"

A single gunshot echoes across the still night; Matthew falls awkwardly to the ground, eyes wide open in shock, a single trickle of blood runs from his left ear. The driver nudges Matthews's body with their soiled stained work boot, turns and walks back to his vehicle. The Ute roars to life, driving slowly past Matthew's lifeless body, shifts gears as tyres spin spewing dirt and dust behind it.

For further updates, pre-orders & awesomeness visit Nicole at
http://spiritualwisdommagazine.com
and her facebook pages
http://facebook.com/spiritualwisdompublishing
http://facebook.com/nicolesuzannebrownauthor
and her Amazon author page.

Printed in Great Britain
by Amazon